Where the Buffalo Roam

Adapted and Illustrated by

Jacqueline Geis

IDEALS CHILDREN'S BOOKS • NASHVILLE, TENNESSEE

Published by Ideals Publishing Corporation
Nashville, Tennessee 37214

Printed and bound in Mexico.

Library of Congress Cataloging-in-Publication Data

Geis, Jacqueline, 1955-

Where the buffalo roam/adapted and illustrated by Jacqueline Geis.

p. cm.

Summary: This expansion of the original verse includes the animals, plants, and geographical features of the American Southwest. Provides additional information on the history of the region and the habits of the wildlife.

ISBN 0-8249-8584-2 (lib. bdg.)—ISBN 0-8249-8570-2 (trade)

1. Animals—Juvenile poetry. 2. West (U.S.)—Juvenile poetry.
3. Children's poetry, American. [1. Desert animals—Poetry. 2. Desert plants—Poetry. 3. Southwest, New—Poetry. 4. American poetry.]
I. Title.

PS3557.E358.W48   1992

811'.54—dc20   92-7733   CIP   AC

The display type was set in Contura Open.
The text type was set in Berkeley Book.
Prehistoric petroglyph ornaments were drawn by the author.
Color separations were made by Blackhawk Color Corporation.

Designed by Joy Chu.

Petroglyphs are carvings or drawings made on rock by prehistoric people. Petroglyphs served early man as markers indicating the location of trails, resources, and water.

THANKS TO PEGGY AND HERB ZARING FOR BELIEVING IN MY ART AND PERPETUATING MY LOVE OF THE SOUTHWEST. AND VERY SPECIAL THANKS TO ROBIN CROUCH.

– J.G.

Dedicated to the land and to a time when the buffalo did roam, when there were no boundaries, and when life was lived with no reservations. — J.G.

Oh, give me a home
Where the buffalo roam
And the deer and the antelope play,

Where seldom is heard
A discouraging word,
And the skies are not cloudy all day.

Oh, show me a land
Where the tall saguaros stand
And the coyotes and jack rabbits run,

Where the Gila lies still,
As the green rat snake will,
In the warmth of the hot morning sun.

Oh, the cottonwoods grow
Where the dry washes flow
And the young javelinas are seen,

And great ridges of rocks
Hide the bighorn sheep flocks
Till they graze on the mountaintops green.

Oh, give me a place
Where the roadrunners race
And the falcons and hummingbirds fly,

Where the dry, desert air
Warms the prickly pear
In the haze of the afternoon sky.

Oh, show me a land
Where the bright diamond sand
Throws its light from the glittering stream,

As the sun slips away
And it gives up the day
To the shaft of the full moon's first gleam.

How often at night,
When the heavens are bright
With the light of the twinkling stars,

Have I stood here amazed
And asked as I gazed
If their glory exceeds that of ours.

Home, home on the range
Where the deer and the antelope play,
Where seldom is heard a discouraging word,
And the skies are not cloudy all day.

THE AMERICAN SOUTHWEST

The watercolor scenes within this book are painted landscapes of the American Southwest, including parts of Arizona, New Mexico, Oklahoma, and Texas, as well as lower regions of Utah, Colorado, and western Kansas. The United States map above is highlighted to show the exact location of the entire featured area.

GLOSSARY

antelope: The fleet-footed pronghorn antelope is not really an antelope. It is a deer. Native to the plains of North America, the pronghorn is greatly reduced in number and endangered in some areas.

bighorn sheep: Desert-dwelling bighorns are lighter in color than those of the Rocky Mountains. Most of these animals live in protected areas.

buffalo: Actually a bison, the buffalo once ranged throughout mainland North America and is now extirpated, which means it no longer lives in the wild. Today, most of the remaining population lives in isolated, western areas of the U.S. and Canada.

cottonwood: The cottonwood is a poplar tree which lines the streams and rivers of the west.

coyote (ki OH tee): Also called a prairie wolf, the wide-ranging coyote runs in a pack. Coyotes dig for water during prolonged droughts, saving many animals with the resulting shallow water pools.

deer: The mule deer ranges from Canada to the plateaus of Mexico. Feeding on grasses and shrubs, it spends the summers in high elevations and moves down for the winter.

dry wash: In the Southwest, another name for a dry wash is arroyo (uh ROY oh). It is a small streambed or gulch which remains dry most of the time. After a heavy rain, the dry wash fills up and flows very fast.

falcon: The widespread use of harmful pesticides took the peregrine falcon near extinction in the 1960s. They were soon classified as endangered, and today there are almost nine hundred breeding pairs of peregrine falcons across the U.S.A.

Gila (HEE la): The Gila monster is the only American poisonous lizard. This lizard falls into a deep stupor during the heat of the day. It winters in a moist burrow, consuming fat stored in its tail.

green rat snake: This little-known reptile is active during the day, except in the heat of the summer, when it is nocturnal. Ranging from eastern Arizona, south through Mexico, and into Costa Rica, the green rat snake is a rare sight in the U.S.

hummingbird: Costa's hummingbird ranges throughout the southern portions of the United States. In the desert, it feeds on the nectar of blossoming cacti and brushes.

jack rabbit: Ranging from the Pacific coast to the Mississippi River, the jack rabbit favors prairies, cultivated land, and arid scrub land.

javelina (hah vuh LEE nuh): Also called a pecarry (PECK uh ree), the javelina neared extinction, but under protection, it has become numerous again in the Southwest. They run in large groups and grunt and bark as though conversing with one another.

prickly pear: Located throughout the Southwest, this cactus provides food and sometimes nesting areas for many desert birds and animals.

roadrunner: Ranging from southern California, Utah, and Kansas and south to Mexico, the roadrunner lives in dry, open places. Capable of flight, this member of the cuckoo family eats cactus fruits, insects, reptiles, and bird's eggs.

saguaro (suh WAHR oh): A protected plant, the saguaro's blossoms, fruits, and structure provide food and shelter for many desert-dwellers. Its white, waxy flowers open at night and close the following afternoon, and its fruits contain juicy, red pulp and hundreds of seeds.

AUTHOR'S NOTE

The origin and author of HOME ON THE RANGE are not known. Edited and adapted repeatedly throughout history, the first-known printing of this poem appeared in a small Kansas newspaper in 1876, under the title *Western Home*.

The closely related *Colorado Home* was printed in 1885, followed by *An Arizona Home* in 1905. Then, in 1908, celebrated song collector John Lomax discovered the lyrics known today, and their music, in San Antonio, Texas.

Lomax brought the song from relative obscurity into national view when including it in his 1910 collection entitled *Cowboy Songs*. By 1933, HOME ON THE RANGE reigned as the most popular song in the nation.

While the official home of these treasured verses is uncertain, they are here adapted to showcase the many faces of the American Southwest, from wide, grassy plains, through harsh-yet-lovely desert, and to the Rocky Mountain foothills.

Concentrating on the desert and its diverse life and landforms, this book features protected, threatened, and endangered species. Bison, pronghorn antelope, and bighorn sheep now live in protected areas, and even the saguaro cactus is not free from danger.

The adaptation of this favorite childhood song simply serves as a backdrop in my own attempt to preserve this magnificent land.